P9-DDT-859

AMAZING
HORSES

AMAZING
HORSES

Sandy Creek
NEW YORK

An Imprint of Sterling Publishing
387 Park Avenue South
New York, NY 10016

SANDY CREEK and the distinctive Sandy Creek logo
are registered trademarks of Barnes & Noble, Inc.

© 2012 by Amber Books Ltd

This 2012 edition is published by Sandy Creek.

All rights reserved. No part of this publication may be reproduced, stored in a retrieval system, or transmitted, in any form or by any means, electronic, mechanical, photocopying, recording, or otherwise, without prior written permission from the publisher.

Editorial and design by
Amber Books Ltd
74–77 White Lion Street
London N1 9PF
United Kingdom

Author: Tom Jackson
Consulting Editor: Per Christiansen
Series Editor: Sarah Uttridge
Editorial Assistant: Kieron Connolly
Designer: Andrew Easton
Picture Research: Terry Forshaw

ISBN 978-1-4351-4274-9

For information about custom editions, special sales, and premium and corporate purchases, please contact Sterling Special Sales at 800-805-5489 or specialsales@sterlingpublishing.com.

Manufactured in China

Lot #:
2 4 6 8 10 9 7 5 3 1
09/12

Contents

Introduction 6

Akhal-Teke 8

American Saddlebred 10

Andalusian 12

Anglo-Arabian 14

Appaloosa 16

Arabian 18

Ardennes 20

Asturcón 22

Belgian Draft 24

Camargue 26

Falabella 28

French Trotter 30

Friesian 32

Galician Pony 34

Haflinger 36

Icelandic Pony 38

Kabardin 40

Karabakh 42

Kentucky Mountain Saddle 44

Knabstrup 46

Konik 48

Lipizzaner 50

Maremmano 52

Miniature Horse 54

Missouri Fox Trotter 56

Morgan 58

Mustang 60

Norwegian Fjord 62

Orlov Trotter 64

Palomino 66

Paso Fino 68

Przewalski's Horse 70

Quarter Horse 72

Sella Italiano 74

Selle Français 76

Shetland Pony 78

Standardbred 80

Suffolk Punch 82

Tennessee Walking 84

Tersk 86

Thoroughbred 88

Trait du Nord 90

Wielkopolski 92

Zweibrücker 94

Glossary/Index 96

Introduction

Horses come in many sizes—they can be miniature or gigantic, wide or narrow, short or long. Some have long, thick manes and tails, others have manes that stick up in the air! There are hundreds of different breeds in the world and every breed has different qualities that make them unique.

Akhal-Teke

This breed is one of the oldest of any type of horse. People were already breeding Akhal-Tekes at least 3,000 years ago. Experts think this breed is very similar to the ancient wild horses that lived in the dry grasslands of Central Asia long before people began to keep domestic horses. Today, the breed is famous for being able to run very long distances.

DID YOU KNOW?

- In a traditional stable, an Akhal-Teke is wrapped in warm felt on cold nights.

- Before a race, trainers feed these horses on eggs, mutton fat, and fried dough.

- The Akhal-Teke horse is the national symbol of Turkmenistan, where most members of this breed still live today.

WHERE DO THEY LIVE?

Akhal-Teke horses come from Turkmenistan, a country in the desert region of Central Asia.

Asia

Turkmenistan

Desert Horse

◀ The Akhal-Teke has thin skin with a coat of short, fine hairs. These stop the horse from getting too hot and bothered while galloping across dry deserts.

FACTS

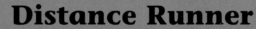

SIZE

● There are about 3,500 Akhal-Teke horses in the world.

● The coat is always a golden brown.

● The breed is just over 15 hands tall.

Distance Runner

▶ Today an Akhal-Teke horse may be a cross-country racer, a show jumper, or a dressage horse. However, it was traditionally used as a hardworking horse. It could carry a person the 2,500 mi (4,020 km) from Ashgabat, the capital of Turkmenistan, to Moscow, in Russia, in 84 days. Crossing deserts, forests, and hills on the way, the horse did not need to rest or feed for long each day.

Tall and Thin

▶ The Akhal-Teke is a large and strong horse, but also a slender one with long legs and a long neck.

American Saddlebred

This is one of the most common breeds in North America. It can be ridden with a saddle or used to pull a carriage. Most American Saddlebreds are black, bay (brown with a black mane), or chestnut, although a few have coats with paler colors.

WHERE DO THEY LIVE?

This breed is found all over North America, but originally came from the state of Kentucky.

USA • Kentucky

High Leg

▶ When American Saddlebreds walk or run, they lift their front legs higher than most other types of horse.

DID YOU KNOW?

⚜ The breed is related to the Narragansett Pacer, the first ever U.S. breed, developed in the eighteenth century and now extinct.

⚜ Many of the horses used in Hollywood movies are American Saddlebreds.

⚜ General Robert E. Lee rode a Saddlebred horse named Traveller in the American Civil War.

FACTS

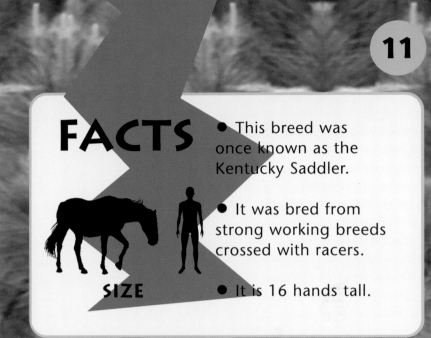

SIZE

● This breed was once known as the Kentucky Saddler.

● It was bred from strong working breeds crossed with racers.

● It is 16 hands tall.

Fancy Footwork

▶ Like all horses, the American Saddlebred can walk, trot, and canter. Each is faster than the one before, with the horse's feet moving in certain patterns. The American Saddlebred has two more ways of moving: the "slow gait" and "rack." These are faster than walking but smoother rides than a trot or a canter.

Sure-Footed

◀ Despite being bred for performing in a show ring, the American Saddlebred is a fast and spirited galloper. If its hooves are clipped short, the breed is ideal for trail riding.

Andalusian

This Spanish breed is one of the most important. Many of the world's other breeds are linked to this ancient athletic type of horse. Most North American breeds are descended from it. Today's Andalusian horses are related to the first domestic breed of horses in Europe. Its ancestors came to Spain more than 11,000 years ago.

WHERE DO THEY LIVE?

Andalusians come from a hot, dry region in southern Spain called Andalusia.

Europe

Spain
●
Andalusia

War Horse

► The strong spirit of an Andalusian horse made it the breed of choice for knights riding into battle.

Bay or Gray

◀ Andalusian horses are normally bay—red-brown with a black mane and tail—or gray. Their manes and tails are long and thick and often have wavy hairs.

FACTS

SIZE

● Andalusians are best used for riding, not for hauling carts.

● The Andalusian is a close relative of the Lipizzaner breed.

● It is 15.2 hands tall.

DID YOU KNOW?

● Some of the best Andalusian horses are bred by Spanish monks.

● The oldest breeding stables, or studs, are in the Spanish cities of Cordoba, Jerez de la Frontera, and Seville.

● The Andalusian is descended from the Sorraia, an ancient pony breed from Portugal.

Power and Grace

▶ The Andalusian is a sturdy horse with thicker legs than most light horses (the breeds that are good at running). The leg joints are also strong. The breed's neck is short and muscular. The neck arches more than those of other breeds, which gives the head a curved, hawklike appearance when seen from the side.

Anglo-Arabian

This breed is a cross between the tough Arabian horse and the high-speed Thoroughbred racehorse from England. As a result it is a fast runner, like a Thoroughbred, but is easier to ride and can also travel long distances without getting tired, like an Arabian.

WHERE DO THEY LIVE?

Despite its name, the Anglo-Arabian is most common in France.

Europe

France

Red-Brown

▶ Most Anglo-Arabian horses are chestnut and bay, which is red-brown with black. A few have paler coats.

DID YOU KNOW?

⊔ The main Anglo-Arabian breeding stables are in Pompadour, in central France.

⊔ Anglo-Arabians are often used in horse trial competitions, which involve racing, jumping, and dressage.

⊔ In France, there are races reserved just for Anglo-Arabian horses.

FACTS

SIZE

● In the USA the Anglo-Arabian is registered as a type of Arabian horse.

● The breed is one of the oldest in France.

● It stands at more than 16 hands tall.

Galloper

◀ The breed has long legs and powerful sloping shoulders. That means the horse can reach forward and take long, leaping strides when galloping.

Crossing Two Breeds

▶ Today's Anglo-Arabian horses are descended from just five ancestors from the 1830s. They were two Arabian stallions that came from Syria named Massoud and Aslam (although this horse may have been from the Akhal-Teke breed) and three Thoroughbred mares—Daer, Comus Mare, and Selim Mare.

Appaloosa

Horses were introduced to the Americas by Spanish explorers about 500 years ago. The Appaloosa was one of the first breeds developed by Native Americans. It is named after the Palouse River of Idaho and Washington, where the Nez Perce Native Americans bred the horses 200 years ago. It is one of the few breeds of horses always to have a spotted coat.

WHERE DO THEY LIVE?

The Appaloosa horse comes from the USA, originally from the Pacific Northwest.

USA ●

DID YOU KNOW?

- The breed was almost wiped out during a war between the Nez Perce and the USA in 1877.

- The Appaloosa is now the third most common breed of horse in the world.

- The Appaloosa is descended from the Spanish horse, similar to the Andalusian breed.

Mane and Tail

▶ The manes and tails of the Appaloosa breed are often, but not always, short and thinly haired.

FACTS

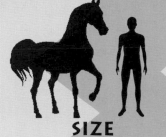

SIZE

• The Appaloosa is a small breed. It measures between 14 and 14.5 hands tall.

• The breed is a hard worker and a good jumper. It is often used for pleasure rides.

Coat Types

◀ There are five Appaloosa coats: leopard (left); blanket (white over the hips); marble (reddish with dark spots); snowflake (spotting on hips); and frost (white spots).

White Eye

▶ As well as having spotty coats, Appaloosa horses are unusual because they have a white area around their eyes—like people do, but unlike other horses. Another unusual feature is that the skin on the horse's small head, especially around the nose, is covered in pale patches.

Arabian

There are few other types of horse that are not connected in some way to this most ancient of breeds. The people of Arabia have been breeding these horses for at least 4,000 years. Coming from a desert, the Arabian has a lot of stamina— it does not tire easily. It is an efficient runner. Its body appears to almost float in midair as its legs gallop away.

WHERE DO THEY LIVE?

Asia

Arabia

As its name suggests, this horse comes from Arabia, a very hot, dry part of the Middle East.

High Tail

▶ The Arabian always runs with its tail held up in a high curve. The silky tail hairs are never trimmed.

DID YOU KNOW?

The USA has the largest population of Arabian horses today.

The World Arabian Horse Organization is in charge of recording the world's Arabian horses.

Arabian cavalry horses were not as fast as European chargers, but were more nimble and controllable during battle.

FACTS

SIZE

● The first Arabian horses are shown in Bedouin artworks from 2000 BCE.

● The Arabian is a medium-sized horse standing between 14 and 15 hands high.

Fewer Bones

◀ The Arabian has just 17 rib bones. That makes it more flexible than other horses, which have 18 ribs. There are also fewer bones at the base of an Arabian's spine and in its tail.

Ideal Breed

▶ The Arabian horse was spread across the world more than 1,000 years ago as the Islamic Empire grew. Wherever it went, local people admired the desert horse's speed and stamina as well as its gentle nature. Arabians were bred with local horses, resulting in many of the breeds we see around the world today.

Ardennes

This is one of the earliest heavy horse breeds. They are huge draft animals, bred to haul plows and carts. They are said to be descendants of the ancient Forest Horse, a wild ancestor that lived in northern Europe. The largest and strongest Ardennes horses are from the north of Belgium. Lighter and faster varieties are found further south.

WHERE DO THEY LIVE?

This large workhorse is named for the Ardennes, a forested area of Belgium.

• Belgium

Europe

Hairy Feet

▶ The Ardennes has thick legs with thick hair around the feet to keep them warm and dry in bad weather.

Quiet Giant

◀ Ardennes horses are huge and powerful but are also very good tempered. That makes it easier and safer for people to control them.

FACTS

SIZE

● Ardennes horses have been used to develop other draft horse breeds, such as Russian Heavy Draft.

● Most Ardennes are bay or roan (white flecks), but can be any color.

DID YOU KNOW?

⊂ The Ardennes was a farming horse, but most of its work is now done by tractors.

⊂ The well-muscled breed is sometimes slaughtered for meat in Belgium, Luxembourg, and France.

⊂ The Ardennes horse was used to haul heavy guns around battlefields.

Short and Sturdy

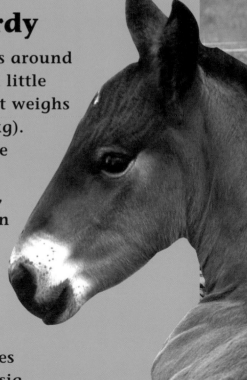

▶ The Ardennes horse is around 15.5–16 hands tall—a little more for stallions—and it weighs 1433–2205 lb (650–1000 kg). In Roman times the horse was much shorter. In the early nineteenth century, French emperor Napoleon Bonaparte crossed the Ardennes with Arabians to boost the breed's stamina. He needed tougher horses to haul artillery for long distances during his attack on Russia.

Asturcón

Also known as the Asturian Pony, this is one of several pony breeds that are based in Iberia (Spain and Portugal). The pony runs in an ambling style, moving both the legs on one side at the same time. This is more comfortable for a rider. The Asturçon was popular as a "hobby horse" for wealthy French and British families in the nineteenth century.

WHERE DO THEY LIVE?

The Asturcón pony comes from the dry and hilly region of northwestern Spain.

Europe

Spain

Dark Horse

▶ The Asturcón is normally black or sometimes bay. The mane and tail are long and flowing.

Body Shape

◀ The breed has a long neck and small head for a pony. However, its large feet help it to walk and run through the rock-covered hills of its homeland.

FACTS

SIZE

- This pony breed never has white markings on the head.

- The pony stands 11.2 to 12.2 hands tall.

- The pony is easy to tame for riding.

DID YOU KNOW?

- The Asturcón is related to the tarpan, a type of extinct wild horse.

- The pony was taken to Ireland several centuries ago and became known as the Irish Hobby breed.

- The Irish Hobby was a cavalry horse used in the many wars between England and Scotland in the thirteenth century.

In the Wild

▶ The Asturcón pony is very rare today. It nearly became extinct—gone forever—in the past, because few of the ponies were kept in stables. Instead they became feral, left to roam wild in the hills of Asturias. Many died in the harsh conditions. Today the few pure Asturcón ponies left are protected for the future.

Belgian Draft

This massive, very strong workhorse has been pulling carts and plows in northern Europe since Roman times. The breed is described as a coldblood. That means it is calm and slow. It is very different to the hotblood breeds related to Arabian horses.

WHERE DO THEY LIVE?

The Belgian Draft comes from the flat farmland region of Belgium.

● Belgium

Europe

Coat Color

▶ Belgian Draft horses are normally chestnut in color and sometimes roan (dark blotches), with flecks of white hair.

Heavy Lifters

◀ A draft horse is one that pulls carts rather than carrying a rider. The Belgian Draft was one of the first heavy horse breeds, and is related to others like the British Shire Horse.

FACTS

SIZE

• The breed is sometimes known as the Brabant after its home region in Belgium.

• These are some of the largest horses in the world, standing up to 19 hands tall.

DID YOU KNOW?

Most of today's Belgian Draft horses are related to three stallions from 150 years ago. They were named Orange 1, Jean 1, and Bayard.

During the Middle Ages, horses of this large breed were used as chargers on the battlefield. They were not very fast but were still hard to stop.

Forest Horse

▶ The Belgian Draft breed is thought to be a close relative to the Forest Horse, a wild ancestor that lived in the cold forests of northern Europe in ancient times. Like its wild relation, the Belgian Draft is happy in wet weather thanks to its thick coat. It also has a long fine mane and feathery hairs over its hooves to keep out the cold. Its short and thick legs help the horse walk over muddy fields or through snow without slipping.

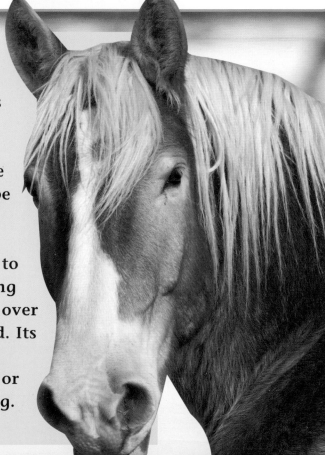

Camargue

Known as "White Horses of the Sea," Camargue horses live in a wetland region of southern France. Horses have been living in this area for thousands of years. There are even Stone Age paintings from 15,000 years ago in nearby caves that show these white or gray horses. In more recent centuries the breed has been crossed with the Barb horse from North Africa.

WHERE DO THEY LIVE?

Camargue horses come from the delta of the Rhône River in the south of France.

Europe
France

Galloping

▶ The Camargue horses gallop around their wetland home in half-wild herds called "manades."

No Outsiders

◀ The Camargue wetland is a very remote place, and no other horse lives there. This is the reason why the Camargue breed has remained so distinctive.

FACTS

SIZE

● At a maximum height of 14.2 hands, this breed is almost small enough to be classified as a type of pony.

● A Camargue's tough hooves do not usually need shoes.

DID YOU KNOW?

⊔ Fossil remains of ancient ancestors of Camargue horses were found in the nineteenth century in central France.

⊔ The Camargue horses graze on salty reeds, which other breeds could not stomach.

⊔ The horses round up the wild Camargue bulls sent to Spain for bullfights.

French Cowboys

▶ The Camargue horses are owned by the "gardians"—the region's cowboys, who raise cattle on the wetlands. Just like the horses, the black cattle live semi-wild, and the tough gardians ride out across the marshes on their white mounts to round up herds. The Camargue is a fast galloper through the shallow water. However, its front legs are farther back on its body than other horses. This means it cannot trot very well, so it only ever walks or runs.

Falabella

This breed is said to be the smallest of any horse. Most pony breeds are small and stocky because it helps them live in cold and hilly places. However, the Falabella has been bred to be a tiny version of a horse, with slim legs and long neck. These little horses are kept as pets. They are too weak for riding but can haul small carriages.

WHERE DO THEY LIVE?

The Falabella comes from a large ranch near Buenos Aires in Argentina.

South America

Argentina

Big Head

▶ The Falabella's head often looks large next to its elegant, horselike body and legs.

Grooming

◀ Falabellas are born with all coat colorings, even spots. The tail and mane grow thick and long and must be groomed and trimmed carefully by the owners.

FACTS

SIZE

● The horse stands at just 7 hands high, making it the smallest recognized breed of horse in the world.

● There are only a few thousand members of this breed alive today.

DID YOU KNOW?

☊ It took nearly 100 years for the Falabella family to produce this breed.

☊ Most Falabella horses live in North America today. They are descended from 12 stallions imported from Argentina in 1962.

☊ In future Falabellas could be used to guide blind people instead of dogs.

Tiny Horse

▶ The Falabella breed takes its name from a family of Argentine breeders who developed it in the twentieth century. The breeders crossed small Shetland ponies with powerful Thoroughbreds to create tiny but lean horses. However, the little breed is often born with weak, thin bones and neck problems.

French Trotter

Developed in the nineteenth century, this breed is one of the best trotting racers in the world. In such a race, the horse pulls a person sitting in a small cart, normally with just two wheels. The horse is only allowed to trot, not gallop, and this breed can trot very quickly indeed.

WHERE DO THEY LIVE?

French Trotters come from Normandy, a farming region in northern France.

Europe
France

DID YOU KNOW?

- The breed is sometimes called a Norman Trotter.

- The three stallions that helped start this breed were named Norfolk Phenomenon, Young Rattler, and Heir of Linne.

- Later French Trotters have been crossed with American Standardbred horses to make the breed faster runners.

Strong Legs

◀ The breed's back legs are very strong, while the front legs are a little thinner. That makes it easier to fit a harness comfortably around the horse's shoulders.

FACTS

SIZE

● This breed stands between 15 and 16.2 hands tall.

● A four-year-old horse can trot 0.6 mi (1 km) in 1 minute, 22 seconds.

Road to Racetrack

▶ The French Trotter is a mix of several earlier breeds, some of which were fast racers, while others were good at pulling carts using a harness. The main breed was the Norman workhorse, which was used by French farmers over many centuries. This was crossed with Norfolk Roadsters, which are trotting horses from England that pull small carriages, and Thoroughbreds, which are the world's fastest and most competitive racing horses.

Solid Color

▶ A French Trotter's coat is always a single, or solid, color. They are most often chestnut, bay, or brown.

Friesian

This breed of horse is well-loved in its homeland in western Europe as a powerful but friendly horse. It is an ancient breed that was used in battles, as a workhorse, and even as a circus performer. The breed has strong links to the ancient Forest Horse, which lived wild in Europe many thousands of years ago.

WHERE DO THEY LIVE?

The Friesian is named for Friesland, a flat farming region in the Netherlands.

Netherlands

Europe

Black Beauty

▶ The Friesian is always black, with a long mane and tail, plus feathering, or thick hairs, over the hooves.

Useful Breed

◀ A Friesian horse is easy to keep. It doesn't require special foods. It also earns its keep well. The breed can be used to haul carts but is also happy to be ridden.

FACTS

SIZE

- A Friesian horse stands at least 15 hands tall.

- The breed's head is very large and held high.

- The breed is also named the Frisian.

DID YOU KNOW?

- Friesians are often used to pull coffins in traditional funeral processions.

- The legions of ancient Rome guarded their sides, or flanks, with squads mounted on Friesian horses.

- Friesians are related to Shires in England and Oldenburgs in Germany.

Carrying Knights

▶ The Friesian was one of the few breeds strong enough to carry a knight in heavy armor. Around 1,000 years ago, hundreds of knights rode these horses to fight the Crusades in the Middle East. In the sixteenth century, the Netherlands was ruled by Spain, and the heavy Friesian breed was crossed with lighter and faster Spanish horses.

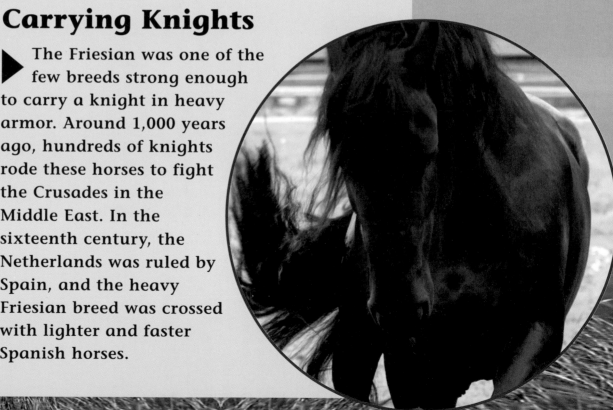

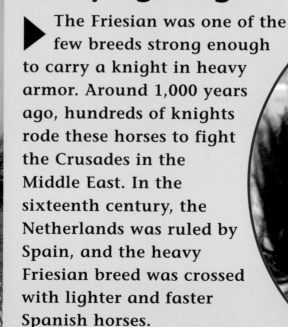

Galician Pony

This small breed lives wild in the hills of northern Spain. The tough ponies have a smooth but very fast walking style. This feature helps the animals in their rugged homeland, and also made them very popular with sixteenth-century breeders.

WHERE DO THEY LIVE?

This pony breed is from Galicia, a wet and windy highland region in northwestern Spain.

Europe

● **Spain**

Hey Shorty

▶ The Galician Pony has short, thick legs and a rounded body. These features help the pony to keep warm.

Long Hair

◀ Herds of ponies were traditionally kept for their long hair. Once a year, herds were driven into a pen and their tails and manes were cut for use in soft brushes.

FACTS

SIZE

● The Galician Pony is generally solid chestnut, but sometimes bay.

● This breed of pony is less than 12 hands tall.

● There are about 20,000 of these ponies.

DID YOU KNOW?

☙ The Galician Pony is an important source of meat in Spain.

☙ Each summer, a pony fair, or curro, is held in the Galician hills, where the semi-wild ponies are branded by their owners.

☙ There are three types of Galician Pony. One of them grows a mustache in old age.

Galiceno

▶ The Galician Pony is a mix of earlier pony breeds brought to the region by the Romans and earlier peoples. The breed was one of the first to be taken to the Americas. They became a very important part of the Galiceno Pony, a modern Mexican breed. The Galiceno is a little bigger and faster than the Galician Pony, probably because it has been crossed with Spanish horse breeds. It is used as a pleasure horse, especially good for young riders.

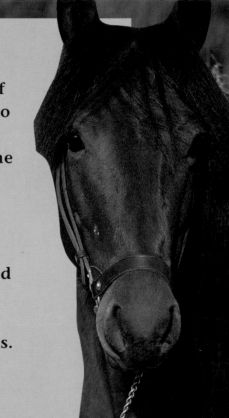

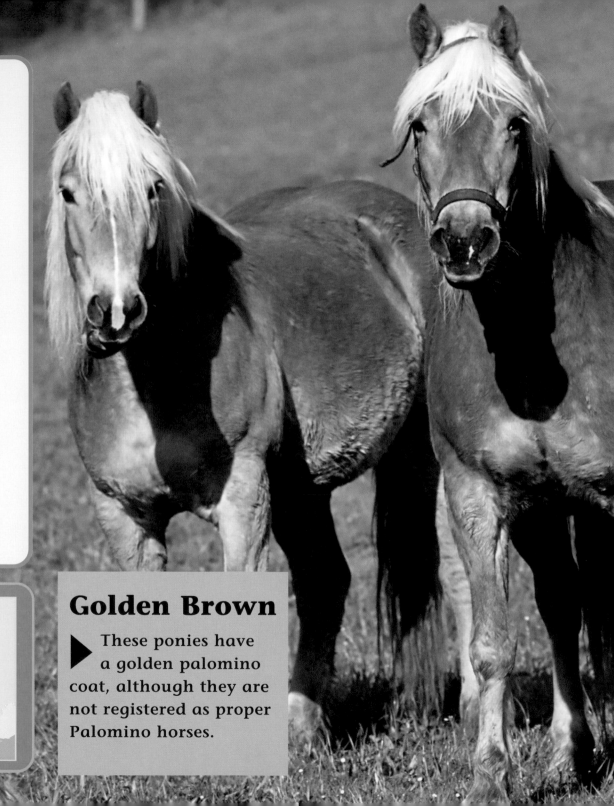

Haflinger

Like most pony breeds, this one comes from a harsh mountain environment. The Haflinger is named for the village of Hafling in Austria, where it has been bred for the last 150 years or so. It is based on an older breed called the Alpine Heavy Horse, but one of its earliest stallions was an Arabian. This cross-breeding gave Haflingers great stamina.

WHERE DO THEY LIVE?

The Haflinger is from the mountainous Tyrol region mainly in Austria but also northern Italy.

Europe
•
Austria
•
Italy

Golden Brown

▶ These ponies have a golden palomino coat, although they are not registered as proper Palomino horses.

Snow Work

◀ The Haflinger is well used to cold weather. One of its jobs is to pull sleds through deep snow. It also pulls carts and is strong enough to carry a rider.

FACTS

SIZE

● Haflingers are quite tall for ponies. Most grow to 14 hands; a few reach 16 hands tall.

● The first horse clone was a Haflinger called Prometea. She was made in a lab in 2003.

DID YOU KNOW?

☞ This breed is sometimes also known as the Edelweiss Pony.

☞ Every pony is branded with a star-shaped Edelweiss flower with an H at its center.

☞ The heavy Polish Huçul and Konik Ponies, as well as some Bosnian breeds, are related to the Haflingers.

Mystery Beginnings

▶ The Haflinger is one of the most successful pony breeds of all. There are at least a quarter of a million living around the world. No one is quite sure where they came from originally. Was the Alpine Heavy Horse another relative of the ancient Forest Horse that lived wild in Europe long before people bred horses? Or was the mountain herd made up of the horses that were left behind in the sixth century by a defeated Goth army from eastern Europe?

Icelandic Pony

The first horses came to Iceland at the end of the ninth century, when Vikings in longboats settled this cold Atlantic island. The ponies that live there now are the direct descendants of those first arrivals. There has been almost no interbreeding for more than 1,000 years.

WHERE DO THEY LIVE?

The pony is found all over Iceland, but its main breeding area is in the north.

Greenland

Iceland

Color Types

▶ There are 15 coat colors for the Icelandic Pony, ranging from pinto (large white patches) to black.

Horse or Pony

◀ Many people regard the Icelandic breed to be a horse, despite easily being small enough to be classed as a pony. The breed is the biggest one in Iceland.

FACTS

SIZE

● Some types of Icelandic Ponies are bred especially for their meat rather than for work or for riding.

● The breed stands between 12.2 and 13.2 hands tall.

DID YOU KNOW?

U The Icelandic breed is based largely on the tough Fjord Pony brought over from Norway.

U Some of the horses brought to Iceland by Vikings would also have come from Ireland and the Scottish islands, which are now home to breeds like the Shetland and Connemara ponies.

Mover and Shaker

▶ The Icelandic Pony is a gaited breed. The word "gait" means a way of moving the legs. Three simple horse gaits are the walk, trot, and canter. The Icelandic breed has two more gaits: a fast walk called the tölt, and a pace, where both legs on each side move at the same time. These extra gaits help with climbing.

Kabardin

This is one of the hardiest mountain breeds in the world, known for being very sure-footed mounts. One Kabardin horse has even carried a rider to the top of Mount Elbrus, Europe's tallest peak! The breed was developed in the mountains of southern Russia about 500 years ago. They are still raised in herds today, left to graze on mountain pastures.

Dark Colors

▶ Kabardins are dark horses. They are always either black or bay—red-brown with a black mane and tail.

WHERE DO THEY LIVE?

The Kabardin horse lives in the Caucasus Mountains between Europe and Asia.

Europe

Caucasus

Asia

Ride and Race

◀ Kabardins are able to haul carts but are best as a saddle horse. The best runners of each year are tested on a racetrack to ensure the breed stays strong.

FACTS

SIZE

● The knees are slightly splayed outward, giving it a bow-legged appearance. That helps the horse to power up steep slopes.

● The Kabardin stands at about 15 hands tall.

DID YOU KNOW?

⊔ An Anglo-Kabardin is a cross between an English Thoroughbred and a Kabardin horse.

⊔ Anglo-Kabardins are larger and faster but do not lose their mountain toughness.

⊔ The breed is named for the Kabardin people of the northern Caucasus. They are also known as Circassians.

Mountainous

▶ The Kabardin is very much a mountain horse. It was developed by crossing tough desert breeds with sure-footed hill ponies. As well as being a good climber, the Kabardin can also find its way around in the dark or misty mountain weather.

Karabakh

This breed from the border region between Asia and Europe is a half mountain horse, half steppe horse. (A steppe is grassland, similar to prairie.) The breed was developed in the seventeenth century by crossing desert horses with mountain breeds, and then adding in some Arabian blood to make them faster runners.

Close Relation

▶ The Karabakh is a slender horse, very similar to the Akhal-Teke breed, which comes from nearby.

WHERE DO THEY LIVE?

The Karabakh horse comes from the southern region of the Caucasus mountains.

Europe

Caucasus
●

Asia

Metallic Coat

◀ The Karabakh's coat is said to be metallic chestnut, because it shimmers in the light. The coat is made of short hairs, so the horse does not get too hot.

FACTS

SIZE

• This slender horse is smaller than most breeds, standing 14 hands tall.

• Some varieties have a paler, dun-colored coat, where fair hairs grow on dark skin.

DID YOU KNOW?

⊌ The best Karabakh horses are raced against each other, mostly in Baku, the capital of Azerbaijan. The winners are sold for large amounts of money.

⊌ This breed is related to the Don, the powerful horses used by the Russian Cossacks cavalry.

Sports Horse

▶ The Karabakh breed is used in several horseback sports, because it is fast yet can turn quickly on the field. The sports include a game called "chaugan," which is similar to polo. (Riders knock a ball with a long club into the other side's goal.) Another Caucasus game is "surpamakh," which is similar to basketball on horseback.

Kentucky Mountain Saddle

This American breed was not well known until the 1980s. Before that the horses were just found in eastern Kentucky, where they were an ideal mount for riding through the rugged landscape.

WHERE DO THEY LIVE?

As its name suggests, the Kentucky Mountain breed is from the U.S. state of Kentucky.

Kentucky

USA ●

Farm Horse

▶ The Mountain Saddle horse was bred by farmers. It is used mainly for riding but can pull carts, too.

Even Temper

◀ The Kentucky Mountain Saddle breed is a good horse to learn to ride on. It is not too big, does what it is told, and does not bounce the rider around too much.

FACTS

SIZE

● The Kentucky Mountain Saddle horse is not a big breed. It must be more than 11 hands, but most are less than 14 hands tall.

● It uses both Western and English saddle styles.

DID YOU KNOW?

⊃ If a horse of this type has more than 36 in (90 cm) of white patches it is classified as a Spotted Mountain Horse.

⊃ The Kentucky Mountain Saddle Horse Association is in charge of recording members of this breed.

⊃ There are more than 20,000 registered members of the breed.

Four-Beat Running Style

▶ When most horses run, their hooves normally produce a three-beat sound pattern. The Kentucky Mountain Horse runs in a smoother style, which produces four beats of sound with every stride. This way of moving is called ambling. Although ambling is not as fast as the gallop of a racehorse, it is much more comfortable for the rider sitting on top.

Knabstrup

Named for the village of Knabstrup in Denmark, this breed is descended from one Spanish mare that was brought there a little over 200 years ago. She gave birth to several spotty horses, and this is the main feature of the breed. Knabstrups look similar to the Appaloosas of North America, but are a completely different European breed.

WHERE DO THEY LIVE?

The Knabstrup, or Knabstruper, breed comes from Denmark in northern Europe.

Europe

Denmark

Long Legs

▶ The Danish breed is athletic with flexible legs that allow it to make long strides when galloping.

DID YOU KNOW?

⊃ Knabstrup horses can have any coat color, but are usually pale with dark spots.

⊃ Like other spotted breeds, Knabstrups also have faint stripes on their hooves.

⊃ These horses are often spotted below the knee, unlike other similar breeds.

FACTS

SIZE

● Knabstrups are around 15 hands tall.

● The breed has a straighter back than the Appaloosas. The withers, or shoulders, also stick up more than in the American breed.

Butcher's Breed

▶ The Knabstrup breed began in 1808 when a Danish breeder bought a Spanish mare from a local butcher. That horse was named Flaebehoppen. She was crossed with stallions of the Frederiksborg breed. Today's Knabstrups are all descended from Flaebehoppen's grandson, who was named Mikkel.

Spot the Horse

◀ Spotty breeds are not new. There are cave drawings that are 30,000 years old showing horses with spots. The Knabstrup got its spots from a breed of Spanish horse.

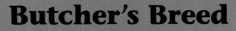

Konik

The name of this breed means "little horse" in Polish. It is only the size of a pony, but does look more like a horse in many ways. For example, it has slender legs and a smaller head than most pony breeds. The Konik has been living in eastern Europe for centuries, and is probably a close relative of the tarpan, a now extinct wild horse that lived in the area.

WHERE DO THEY LIVE?

The Konik is most often found in the farmland and forests of south and east Poland.

Europe

• Poland

Dun Coat

▶ The Konik has a dun-colored coat. That is a brownish-gray covering made from a mix of hair colors.

DID YOU KNOW?

⊂ All tarpans are now dead. The last ones were tamed by Polish farmers around 200 years ago—and bred with Koniks.

⊂ Feral herds of Koniks live in Poland's Bialowieza Forest. (Feral means a farm animal or pet that has gone wild.)

⊂ There are just 600 pure Konik horses alive today.

FACTS

SIZE

• The Konik stands around 13 hands tall, which is very small for a horse breed.

• Koniks often have a dark stripe along their backs, which shows they are related to the tarpan.

Arab Blood

◀ In the last few centuries, Konik breeders have crossed their horses with Arabians. That makes them stronger and able to keep working for a long time.

Put to Work

▶ The Konik is a quiet and hardworking breed. It is a little too small for riding—although it can carry children. Because the breed has wide, upright shoulders, a harness fits it very well. Koniks have been kept for pulling plows and carts for many centuries.

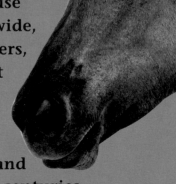

Lipizzaner

This elegant breed of horses are world-famous for being trained to dance at the Spanish Riding School in Vienna, Austria. However, the breed is not Spanish—or Austrian. Instead, these white horses come from the hills of Slovenia in southeastern Europe. They have been bred there for more than 400 years, originally from horses brought from Spain.

WHERE DO THEY LIVE?

The Lipizzaner breed is named for the village of Lipica in Slovenia where they are bred.

Europe

● **Slovenia**

Off-White

▶ No horse is really white. Breeders describe Lipizzaners as gray, because they have small dark patches.

Performers

◀ Lipizzaner horses put on shows all around the world. They are trained at the Vienna School, which is located inside a palace built in the eighteenth century.

FACTS

SIZE

● This breed has very sturdy legs to help with its dance moves, which are often on two legs.

● The Lipizzaner is a large breed. It is generally between 15 and 16 hands tall.

DID YOU KNOW?

Lipizzaner foals are born black. They become gray as they get older.

Most Lipizzaners trained in the Spanish Riding School are now raised at an Austrian stable.

The dances performed by the horses were originally strengthening exercises to prepare the horse for battle.

Royal Breeder

▶ The Lipizzaner breed was begun by Archduke Charles II, the ruler of Austria, in 1580. He imported 33 of the finest Spanish horses—nine stallions and 24 mares—to his ranch in what is now Slovenia. He wanted to have beautiful horses in his palace stables to show off to guests.

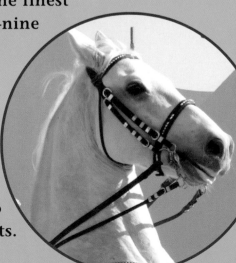

Maremmano

This tough breed of workhorse is thought to be descended from ancient horses from North Africa, Spain, and Arabia, which were brought to Italy over the centuries by many traders and invading armies. However, 200 years ago, the breed was crossed with English horses, such as the Norfolk Roadster, which made it a faster and smoother runner.

WHERE DO THEY LIVE?

The Maremmano breed is named for a grassy region of Tuscany in western Italy.

Europe

Italy

Dark Colors

► All Maremmanos have a solid coat color. Most are dark brown or bay, but some are born gray or roan.

DID YOU KNOW?

⊂ The Maremmano breed is used today by the Italian police force.

⊂ This breed was involved in the last cavalry charge in history. In 1942 an Italian horseback unit attacked the Russian army—and won.

⊂ Modern Maremmanos are fast but not as tough as the original breed.

FACTS

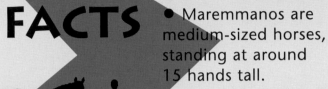

● Maremmanos are medium-sized horses, standing at around 15 hands tall.

● The breed is best used for riding across open country, but it also hauls carts on roads.

SIZE

Cow Herder

▶ The Maremmano is used by *butteri*—Italian herders or cowboys. They round up the long-horned cattle that graze in large herds on the prairies of Tuscany. The butteri must ride close to the huge wild cattle to herd them with long sticks.

Off the Trail

◀ Maremmano horses are very tough and happy to live just about anywhere. It spends long periods outdoors in all sorts of weather.

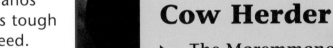

Miniature Horse

Mountain horses are naturally smaller than those that live in deserts or forests. However, breeders can produce horses of any size, very big or very small. Miniature horses come in many breeds. Anything less than 9.5 hands is normally said to be a miniature horse.

WHERE DO THEY LIVE?

Miniature horses live all over the world. The first ones were bred in France and Austria.

Europe

France   Austria

Long Life

▶ Miniature horses live longer than larger ones. However, this might be because they are not work horses, but pets.

DID YOU KNOW?

The smallest horse on record was Thumbelina. She was just 4 hands tall.

Miniature horses are also called mini horses, midget ponies, or pygmy horses.

Many miniature horses are related to the Shetland Pony, a small but very strong Scottish breed.

FACTS

SIZE

- For a horse to be registered as a miniature horse, it will normally be less than 38 in (97 cm) tall.

- The height is measured to the lower end of the mane.

Horses or Ponies?

▶ Small horses are generally called ponies. Ponies are also chunkier than horses, with shorter legs. However, the breeders of some miniature horses try to make their animals look more like a lean, slender horse—just a very small one.

Companions

◀ Miniature horses are kept as pets. They are too small to ride or haul a cart. Instead they make good companions and are bred to be friendly and tame.

Missouri Fox Trotter

The unusual name for this breed comes from the unique fast sliding walk. The breed was produced by crossing fast-running, spirited horses with calmer, sure-footed ones. The result was a very capable horse used by American settlers setting up farms in the Midwest about 200 years ago.

WHERE DO THEY LIVE?

This breed comes from the Ozark Hills, which are mainly in Missouri but also cross into Arkansas.

USA **Missouri**
●
●
Arkansas

Sure-Footed

▶ The Missouri Fox Trotter has strong hooves and powerful hind legs that help it move quickly but safely.

Western Rider

◀ Missouri Fox Trotters are usually ridden rather than harnessed to a carriage. Their wide body is best suited to the Western saddle and bridle.

FACTS

SIZE

● Most Missouri Fox Trotters are chestnut in color but can be born with any color coat.

● The breed is a very big but gentle horse, standing up to 17 hands tall.

DID YOU KNOW?

This breed is a mix of Morgans, Thorough-breds, and Saddlebreds crossed with the Tennessee Walking Horse.

When fox trotting, the horse moves at about 5–8 mph (8–13 km/h), but can double this at top speed.

The breed has been official since 1948.

Sliding Fox Trot

▶ The Missouri Fox Trotter is a gaited breed. A gait is the way an animal moves. All horses can walk, trot, canter, and gallop, but a gaited breed can move in other ways. A Fox Trotter has a sliding gait, where the front legs are walking very fast, and the back legs slide far forward under the body, before pushing the animal forward at high speed. This gait looks unusual but is a very smooth ride. The breed does not need to be trained; it runs like this naturally.

Morgan

This American breed is named after a single stallion. The horse, born in West Springfield, Massachusetts, in the early 1790s, was bought by Justin Morgan, a Vermont school teacher. The powerful stallion was named for him and put to work on the Morgan farm. All Morgans are descended from this one great horse.

WHERE DO THEY LIVE?

Morgans are a North American horse, originally from the state of Vermont.

USA • **Vermont**

Never Gray

▶ Morgans are born with coats of almost all colors, although there are no solid gray Morgans.

Mystery Horse

◀ It is suggested that the first Morgan's father was either an English Thoroughbred, a Friesian horse from Germany, or a Welsh cob. No one knows for sure.

FACTS

SIZE

● Over the years the breed has become more athletic compared to the stocky original.

● The Morgan is a medium-sized breed. It stands between 14.2 and 15.2 hands tall.

DID YOU KNOW?

Ս Morgans were once farm horses but are now used in horse shows, competing in dressage and carriage races.

Ս It is likely that the Morgan breed contains some Arabian blood.

Ս Competing Morgans have longer hooves so they lift up their legs high during shows.

Celebrity Stallion

▶ Justin Morgan is one of the most famous horses in history. There is a statue of him at the Morgan Horse Farm run by the University of Vermont. Until the invention of tanks and trucks, most U.S. mounted soldiers rode on Morgans. Like the original Morgan, they are well-behaved, intelligent, and very strong horses. They can haul heavy loads, pull carts, and also be ridden for long distances without getting too tired.

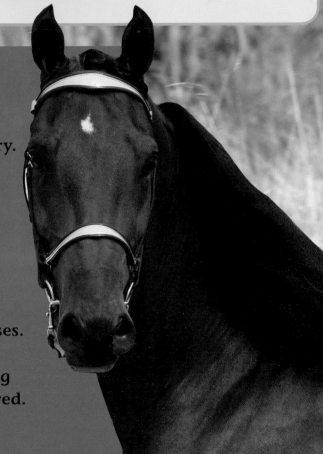

Mustang

This is one of the most famous breeds of horses in the world. They are descended from the first horses brought to North America in the sixteenth century, which escaped to live wild. The word "mustang" comes from the Spanish word *mesteña*, which means "herd." About 100 years ago, there were one million mustangs living wild.

WHERE DO THEY LIVE?

Mustangs come from the West, spreading from northern Mexico to Oregon.

● USA

● Mexico

Spanish Mane

▶ Mustangs have long, flowing manes and tails, which show they are related to Spanish horses.

On the Range

◀ Mustang herds are most at home on the wide-open prairies, which are similar to the Mongolian grasslands from where the first horses came.

FACTS

SIZE

● The Mustang is one of the breeds that was used to create the Quarter Horse.

● The Mustang varies in size. It can be anywhere from 13 to 15 hands tall.

DID YOU KNOW?

⌣ Feral mustangs were captured and tamed by Native Americans living on the prairies.

⌣ Although primitive horses had once lived in North America, they died out more than 10,000 years ago.

⌣ Feral mustangs can range up to 50 miles (80 km) a day.

Wild Horses

▶ Mustangs are feral, which means they are domestic animals that have gone wild again. Some are very fast runners, but they are also often bad-tempered and hard to tame. Throughout the twentieth century, thousands of Mustangs were shot by farmers clearing land for cattle and sheep ranches. By the 1970s, the number of Mustangs had fallen so low that the breed had to be protected by law.

62

Norwegian Fjord

This tough little breed of horse was developed by the Vikings, who spread it to Scotland and Iceland. The horse was used for carrying loads and pulling plows. It is still better than a tractor on the steep slopes above fjords—narrow sea inlets that are surrounded by cliffs.

WHERE DO THEY LIVE?

The Norwegian Fjord breed comes from the coast of Norway, which is famous for its fjords.

Norway
•
Europe

Hair Cut

▶ Following a Viking tradition, the horses' coarse manes are cut short so they form a ridge of bristles.

Small Ears

◀ The Norwegian Fjord has smaller ears than other horses. This helps the animal stay warm in the Norwegian winter. Big ears would freeze in the extreme cold.

FACTS

SIZE

- The breed has short legs, which help it climb up steep, rocky tracks.

- It is short enough to be classified as a pony.

- The breed is between 13 and 14 hands tall.

DID YOU KNOW?

 Most Norwegian Fjord horses are dun in color. This means they have yellow hairs growing on black skin.

The stripe on the back shows up as dark hairs in the middle of the mane.

This breed of horse would have traveled on long sea voyages with Viking raiders.

Ancient Relatives

▶ Norwegian Fjord horses have a dark stripe down their backs, and faint zebra-like bars on their legs. This shows that this breed is descended from Przewalski's Horse. This is an ancient Asian breed, and the only truly wild horse that survives today. Wild herds from Siberia migrated to Norway many thousands of years ago, where they were captured and tamed.

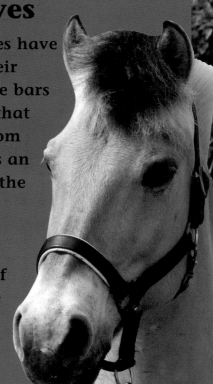

Orlov Trotter

This tall and slender breed was the personal project of Count Alexei Orlov. In eighteenth-century Russia, only a nobleman was allowed to own enough land to breed horses. The Orlov Trotter is a good worker, and stallions were sent all over the country to improve local breeds.

WHERE DO THEY LIVE?

The Orlov Trotter was bred at the Khrenov ranch in the west of Russia.

Russia

Light Draft

 Orlov Trotters are able to pull small carts and carriages. They are also often used to haul snow sleds.

Trot Along

◀ A trotter is a horse that can trot very quickly, while pulling a cart. A cart pulled by a trotting horse moves more smoothly than if it were hauled by a cantering one.

FACTS

SIZE

- Orlov Trotters are normally gray or black.

- The breed stands about 16 hands tall.

- Some Orlov Trotters have long and thin legs that are injured easily.

DID YOU KNOW?

By the nineteenth century, the Orlov Trotter was said to be the fastest harness breed in Europe.

The breed has a long curving neck, which is held high above the harness.

A Russian Trotter is an Orlov Trotter crossed with an American Standardbred.

Russian Breeding

▶ Count Orlov started his breeding program in 1778. He began with a white Arabian stallion and crossed it with many other breeds. The Norfolk Trotter was used to make the breed trot quickly; Dutch horses gave it a calm temperament; Danish ones provided elegance; and Thoroughbreds passed on their great staying power.

Palomino

This type of horse is not a normal breed, but really describes horses with an unusual golden coat color. Members of several breeds, such as Quarter Horses and American Saddlebreds, can also be described as Palominos if they have the distinctive coat. Palomino has been a recognized color for around 400 years.

WHERE DO THEY LIVE?

Palomino horses are usually American. The color was introduced from Spain in the 1500s.

USA ●

Golden Coat

▶ A Palomino has a golden coat and a silvery tail and mane. Any white markings must be below the knee.

DID YOU KNOW?

- Trigger, the faithful horse of Hollywood cowboy Roy Rogers, was a Palomino.

- Mr Ed, a talking horse from a 1960s TV show, was also a Palomino, but he was only ever seen in black and white.

- A chocolate palomino has a dark coat but a silvery-yellow mane and tail.

FACTS

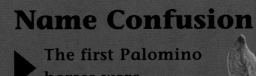

SIZE

- A Palomino can be any height but only horses between 14 and 16 hands are registered.

- To breed a Palomino it is best to cross a chestnut with a cream or albino horse.

Parents

◀ An official Palomino horse has to have at least one Palomino parent, with the other being either a Quarter Horse, Arabian, or Thoroughbred.

Name Confusion

▶ The first Palomino horses were introduced to North America by Spanish settlers. The name Palomino is either taken from a type of yellow grape that grows in Spain or it comes from Juan de Palomino, a Spanish don, or lord. The color is often confused with gray and light chestnut.

Paso Fino

The term *paso fino* means "fine pace" in Spanish, and refers to how this breed can walk very fast. It lifts its front and back legs up very high and very quickly, almost as if it were dancing. No other horse does this and it makes the Paso Fino a very comfortable horse to ride over rough ground. These horses are sometimes termed simply Paso or Criollo.

WHERE DO THEY LIVE?

The Paso Fino breed comes from the islands and mainland around the Caribbean Sea.

● USA

Caribbean
●

Fine Horse

▶ A Paso Fino makes a good horse for trail riding. Many are kept for competitions and shows.

Paso Races

◀ These horses can reach speeds of 30 mph (48 km/h). Paso races are held especially for the breed. Competitions show off the best pacer.

FACTS

SIZE

● The Paso Fino is similar to the "fox trotter" breeds.

● The breed is quite small and slight. It stands at about 14 hands, but is strong enough to carry a rider.

DID YOU KNOW?

U The Paso Fino is a mix of the Andalusian breed from Spain and the Barb from North Africa.

U Local breeders say that a Paso Fino with spirit and drive has "brio."

U The breed is also common in Colombia, and is a close relative of the Paso horse originally from Peru.

New World Breed

▶ The Paso Fino is descended from the horses that were brought to the Americas by Spanish settlers in the early sixteenth century. Today, Puerto Rico in the Caribbean is one of the main breeding centers for the horse. However, the breed now lives all over the world, especially in North and South America.

Przewalski's Horse

This small Mongolian horse is the only wild type of horse left alive today. Even so, it is so rare that it has to be protected in nature reserves. Biologists, the scientists who study animals, think that fast-running light horses, such as Arabians, are descended from this subspecies.

WHERE DO THEY LIVE?

Przewalski's horse lives in the grass-covered hills of Mongolia in Asia.

Asia

• Mongolia

Short Mane

▶ This subspecies has a dun coat (yellow hair) and a short dark mane. There is no forelock of hair over the head.

Long Name

◀ The name is pronounced psheh-val-ski's. It is named for a Polish army officer who came across a wild herd in Mongolia in 1881.

FACTS

SIZE

● The horse's small eyes make its big head look especially large.

● A black stripe runs along the back.

● It is between 12 and 14 hands tall.

DID YOU KNOW?

∪ Przewalski's horse is from the Tachin Schah Mountains of Mongolia. Tachin Schah means the "Mountains of the Yellow Horse."

∪ Przewalski's horse is a different subspecies from other horse and pony breeds.

∪ It is also named the Asian Wild Horse.

Wild Relatives

▶ Przewalski's horse is one of four wild animals from which today's horses were developed. While Arabians and similar breeds came from Przewalski's horse; large ponies were developed from the sturdy tarpan, which lived in eastern Europe; heavy horse breeds, such as the Ardennes, are descended from the Forest Horse, which lived in the north; finally, the Tundra Horse may be related to small ponies.

Quarter Horse

This is thought to be the most common breed of horse in the world. There are more than three million registered. The Quarter Horse is an American breed developed from breeds brought from England and Spain. It has been a valued workhorse since the 1700s.

WHERE DO THEY LIVE?

The Quarter Horse is found all over North America, especially in the west.

North America

Sprinter

▶ The Quarter Horse has very powerful back legs and can outrun any breed over a short distance.

Short Races

◀ The breed has a very large rump, or quarters. However, it gets its name from the short racing events, over about a quarter of a mile, that were held by American settlers.

FACTS

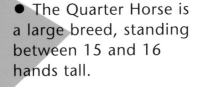

SIZE

● The Quarter Horse is a large breed, standing between 15 and 16 hands tall.

● The neck is long but the head is short and wide compared to other racing breeds.

DID YOU KNOW?

⚲ The Quarter Horse was used by many of the Wild West cowboys for herding cattle.

⚲ The large back legs mean this breed can spring forward and reach full speed very quickly.

⚲ Newer breeds of Quarter Horse have been bred with Thoroughbreds to be even faster runners.

Mixed Breed

▶ The Quarter Horse was developed from the best European horses brought by settlers. Fast English horses were brought to Virginia in the early seventeenth century. These were bred with the hardworking Spanish horses that had arrived the century before. The result was the Quarter Horse.

Sella Italiano

This is a modern breed of Italian horse. Its name means "Italian saddle horse," and it is bred for trail riding, show jumping, and dressage competitions. Horses in the breed are not all related. Instead they qualify for the breed through a series of tests.

WHERE DO THEY LIVE?

Sella Italiano horses are found all over Italy including the island of Sardinia.

Europe

Italy

Three Years

 A horse can only be included in the Sella Italiano breed after the age of three years old.

DID YOU KNOW?

- Almost three-quarters of the horses registered as Sella Italiano are related to English Thoroughbred horses.

- Other common breeds included in the list are Anglo-Arabs and Arabians.

- The performance test for checking breed members is updated every year.

FACTS

SIZE

- The minimum height for a Sella Italiano horse is 61 in (156 cm), or about 15.3 hands.

- The register of Sella Italiano horses is kept by the Italian government.

No Spots

◀ A Sella Italiano horse can be any color—most are dark browns and chestnut. However, only solid colors are allowed. Any horse with spots is disallowed.

Local and Foreign

▶ Many of the horses in the Sella Italiano breed are related to local horse types such as Maremmano, Persano, or Salernitano. However, they can also be born from breeds from elsewhere. As long as they grow large enough and meet the right standard they can be described as a Sella Italiano horse.

Selle Français

This French breed has been developed over the last 150 years or so into one of the best competition horses in the world. It is best suited to carrying a rider, and has a good mix of strength, jumping ability, and speed. The name means "French saddle horse."

WHERE DO THEY LIVE?

The Selle Français breed is found all over France, but is mainly from the Normandy region.

Europe

● **France**

Thick Legs

▶ The Selle Français must have long legs. The lower bone must be more than 8 in (20 cm).

Racing Horse

◀ The Selle Français is often used in cross-country races. They must jump over large obstacles and run through shallow pools and up and down hills.

FACTS

SIZE

- The Selle Français stands 16 hands tall.

- It is a close relation of the French Trotter.

- The breed is not closely related to the American Saddlebred.

DID YOU KNOW?

- The breed's full name is Le Cheval de Selle Français.

- Many of the Selle Français horses of today are related to a few Thoroughbred stallions named Furioso, Orange Peel, and Ibrahim.

- The horses are usually bay and chestnut, and sometimes roan.

Norman Stock

▶ The Selle Français breed was begun in the nineteenth century from sturdy Norman horses. Members of this breed are easygoing and large. They were then crossed with Arabian horses to make them stronger and braver. Next the horses were mixed with Thoroughbreds, which made them faster runners. After World War II (1939–1945), the breed was improved further with Trotter horses and Anglo-Arabs.

Shetland Pony

For its size, this little pony breed is probably the strongest of any type of horse. Even though it is barely 3 ft (1 m) tall, this horse can carry a full-sized man on its back. The breed is best suited for pulling carts, but they are frequently used to give children fun rides.

WHERE DO THEY LIVE?

The Shetland Pony comes from a group of islands called Shetland off northern Scotland.

Shetland Islands

UK

Europe

Rain Coat

▶ The Shetland Pony's long, fine mane gives it protection against the wind and rain on its island home.

Cold Weather

◀ The Shetland is adapted to the cold by being very sturdy with short legs, a compact, round body, and a thick, shaggy coat.

FACTS

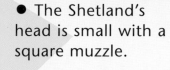

SIZE

● The Shetland's head is small with a square muzzle.

● Most of these ponies stand at around 9 hands tall.

● They live for 30 years.

DID YOU KNOW?

- In the nineteenth century, the Shetland Pony was often used to haul carts along small mining tunnels.

- The American Shetland is a much larger breed developed in the twentieth century, only distantly related to the little Scottish one.

- Shetland Ponies are often used in circuses.

Ancient Breed

▶ Horses have been living on the bleak islands of Shetland, northeast of Scotland, for perhaps 10,000 years. No one is sure, but the ancient relatives of the Shetland Pony might have been a type of Tundra Horse. This wild breed is thought to have lived in the treeless tundra but is now extinct— none of them survives today.

Standardbred

The name of this American breed of horse shows how it is different from the American Saddlebred. Unlike that breed, this one was developed for pulling carriages with a harness—often in races. There are 30 million harness race fans in North America. Most of the time they are watching Standardbreds in action, the fastest harness horses around.

WHERE DO THEY LIVE?

The Standardbred is found all over North America, but is originally from New York State.

North America

● **New York**

Big Rump

▶ Unlike other breeds, the Standardbred's rump or croup is so powerful it is taller than the shoulders.

Standards

◀ Every member of the Standardbred breed must meet a minimum standard speed. Each one should be able to run 1 mile (1.6 km) in 1 minute, 55 seconds.

FACTS

SIZE

● Many of the best Standardbreds are pacers, not trotters. Pacing is when the legs on one side move forward together.

● The Standardbred is about 15 hands tall.

DID YOU KNOW?

U The Standardbred is influenced by the Norfolk Roadster, a trotting horse, and the Narragansett Pacer, a pacing breed.

U The register of Standardbreds was started in 1879.

U Standardbreds are more common in the eastern part of North America.

Messenger Horse

▶ The Standardbred can be traced back to an English Thoroughbred stallion called Messenger, who arrived in America in 1788. The whole of the breed is descended from Hambletonian 10, a stallion related to Messenger. Between 1851 and 1875, Hambletonian 10 had 1,335 offspring.

Suffolk Punch

This is the oldest heavy horse breed in England. It has been developed over 500 years for pulling heavy carts and plows. It was officially recognized as a breed in the eighteenth century. All of the Suffolk Punches alive today are related to a single stallion that was born in 1768.

WHERE DO THEY LIVE?

The Suffolk Punch comes from the county of Suffolk in southeastern England.

**Suffolk
England**

●

Europe

"Fat Fellow"

▶ In old-fashioned English, a "punch" was a funny fat man. This breed is named for its rounded body.

DID YOU KNOW?

- The first Suffolk Punch stallion was called Horse of Ufford.

- The breed is linked to the Norfolk Roadster from the English county to the north of Suffolk.

- Experts think that the Suffolk Punch breed is descended from the Flanders horse, a giant breed from Belgium.

FACTS

SIZE

- The giant horse stands more than 16 hands tall.

- Unlike other heavy horses, this breed's feet are not hairy so they can walk through mud without getting dirty.

Powerful Puller

▶ The Suffolk Punch is bred for hauling. Apart from being very large and wide, the breed has low shoulders compared to a horse bred for racing and riding. That helps a collar harness fit comfortably around the neck. The horse's neck is very thick indeed and the body is low and barrel-shaped.

Unique Color

◀ The horses always have a "chesnut" coat. This is *chestnut* spelled wrong. Even so, the word is still used by the Suffolk Horse Society that registers the breed.

Tennessee Walking

Lovers of this American breed say that they provide the smoothest ride of any horse. The smoothness comes from its unusual gaits, or ways of walking and running. These do not make a rider bounce even at high speeds. One of the gaits is the "running walk."

WHERE DO THEY LIVE?

The breed originally comes from the state of Tennessee in the southern USA.

USA
Tennessee

Smooth Ride

▶ As well as the running walk, this breed has a slow, flat walk and a faster rocking-chair canter.

DID YOU KNOW?

- The Tennessee Walking Horse is often referred to simply as a "Walker."

- English Thoroughbreds have been mixed into the breed to make them faster movers.

- The Tennessee Walking Horse Breeders and Exhibitors' Association is in charge of recording the breed.

FACTS

SIZE

- The Tennessee Walking Horse is a tall but slender horse measuring between 15 and 16 hands tall.

- The breed is very good-natured and popular with families.

All American

▶ The Tennessee Walking Horse was originally developed in the nineteenth century by plantation owners for riding around their large farms. The breed is a mix of several earlier American ones, including the Standardbred, Morgan, and American Saddlebred.

Clicking Teeth

◀ When the horse uses its running walk, it rocks its head back in time with the feet. That keeps the back steady as the horse moves and also makes the teeth click.

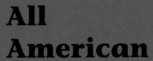

Tersk

Compared to most breeds, the Tersk is quite a modern type of horse. It was bred in the 1930s in the Caucasus Mountains of southern Russia. The breed is named for one of the studs, or breeding stables, where it was raised. Breeders crossed the fast-running Orlov Trotter with Arabians and Anglo-Arabs. The result was (the Tersk) a very large but also elegant breed.

WHERE DO THEY LIVE?

The Tersk breed comes from southwestern Russia in the Caucasus Mountains.

Europe

Caucasus • Asia

Big Gray

▶ Tersks are usually gray and roan. Occasionally chestnut-colored foals are born.

Cold Climate

◀ A Tersk grows a thick coat in the autumn to help it through the winter. It is also cared for by humans, otherwise it wouldn't be able to surive the harsh winter climate.

FACTS

SIZE

● The Tersk is a tall and slender breed.

● It reaches between 14.3 and 15 hands tall.

● The foreleg of a Tersk must be at least 7.5 in (18 cm) long.

DID YOU KNOW?

⌣ The Tersk breed was started by Marshal S.M. Budyonny, an officer in the Red Army (the name of the Russian military at the time).

⌣ The Tersk is a long distance racer. It competes in races hundreds of miles long.

⌣ The breed was officially recognized in 1948.

Breeding Heritage

▶ The Tersk breed comes from two Arabian stallions that belonged to a famous stud in the Ukraine. The stallions, Tsenitel and Tsilindr, were all that remained of that group. They were taken to the Tersk stable to make sure their breed did not die out. There the horses were crossed with Russian breeds, such as Dons and Karbardins, creating the Tersks.

Thoroughbred

A Thoroughbred horse is a racing machine. It is bred to carry a rider around grass and sand racetracks and over high jumps. Thoroughbreds are the most expensive breed of horse. The best stallions earn their owners millions of dollars breeding with other horses, often from other breeds. The many foals they produce will have the Thoroughbred's speed and strength.

WHERE DO THEY LIVE?

The Thoroughbred is found all over the world, but it was originally an English breed.

England

Europe

Long Legs

▶ The Thoroughbred has longer legs than similar breeds. The foot bone is at least 8 in (20 cm) long.

Racehorse

◀ Thoroughbreds run in the biggest races in the world. In a flat race, the horses race on a flat surface. In a steeplechase, they must jump over high fences while racing.

FACTS

SIZE

• A Thoroughbred stands between 16 and 16.2 hands.

• The breed has shoulders that slope back so the front leg can stretch forward to make huge strides.

DID YOU KNOW?

The first important Thoroughbred stallion was born in 1689. Its name was Byerley Turk.

These are courageous horses and will always run as fast as possible. However, that means they tire out easily.

The highest price paid for a Thoroughbred so far is $16 million.

Heritage Breed

▶ The Thoroughbred was developed in England over the seventeenth and eighteenth centuries. The main breeding center today is the town of Newmarket in Suffolk in the east of the country. The breed was formed from English and Irish "running horses"—any fast steed. These were crossed with Arabian and Spanish breeds to add staying power.

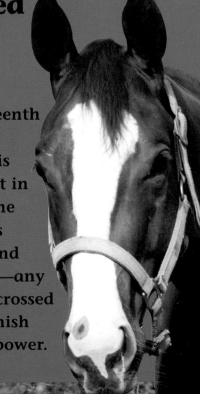

Trait du Nord

This breed includes some of the largest horses in the world. They can measure 68 in (173 cm) to the withers, or shoulders, and weigh more than a ton. The breed was developed over the last 150 years both as a supply of meat and as heavy draft horses.

WHERE DO THEY LIVE?

The Trait du Nord horse is Hainaut in Belgium.

● **Belgium**

Europe

Waiting Time

▶ Horses are only registered with this breed once they are 30 months old, and they must be 16 hands tall.

DID YOU KNOW?

- Trait du Nord horses were at their largest in the 1930s when people ate more horse meat than they do today.

- Today the number of Trait du Nords is low because fewer people eat them and tractors have replaced them on farms.

- There are only a few hundred of these horses alive today.

FACTS

SIZE

- Every year the best Trait du Nord horse is given a prize in Paris.

- The horses stand around 17 hands tall.

- All Trait du Nords are branded with an N.

Mine Worker

◀ The breed has a very wide body, which makes it easier to fit a collar harness. In the past these horses were used to haul coal carts at mines in the region.

New Breed

▶ The term Trait du Nord means "northern type." The breed is registered by the French authorities. This breed was once listed as a type of Ardennes, which is another heavy breed in the area. In 1903, the horses from Hainault, Belgium, which were particularly large, were recognized as a new breed and renamed Trait du Nord.

Wielkopolski

This large, handsome breed is a very useful horse from the farmlands of Poland. It makes a great trail rider, can pull carriages, and is a hardworking farm horse. The Wielkopolski has a good temperament and is easy to control. The horse is also a comfortable ride with a long, striding walk, a smooth trot, and a fast canter and gallop.

WHERE DO THEY LIVE?

The Wielkopolski is found mainly in the flat region of western and central Poland.

Poland
Europe

Best of Both

▶ The Polish breed is elegant and spirited for fast running but also sturdy and strong for hard work.

DID YOU KNOW?

- There are two main groups of Wielkopolski horses. One is light for riding and jumping; the other is heavier and used for pulling loads.

- Another Polish breed is the Malopolski. It comes from the "Little Poland" region in the east.

- The Wielkopolski is always a solid color.

FACTS

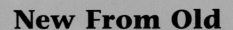

SIZE

- The Wielkopolski is a big breed, standing around 16 hands tall.

- The shoulders slope like a Thoroughbred to help with galloping, but the Polish breed's legs are much thicker.

New From Old

▶ The Wielkopolski breed is the result of a cross between two older Polish breeds: the Poznan from the central region and the Masuren from the west. Both of these breeds are now extinct. Both were a mix of tough local breeds with Arabian and Thoroughbred blood added to make them faster.

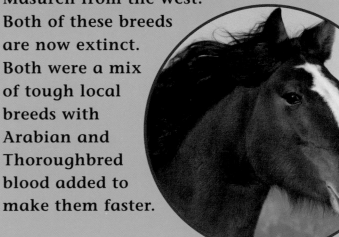

All in a Name

◀ The breed is named for the Wielkopolska region of Poland. That name means "Greater Poland" and refers to a land of lakes and fields in the center of the country.

Zweibrücker

This German breed is one of the best sports horses in the world. Its members are frequently champions in show jumping, dressage, and other horse trial events. The breed was started in 1755 by Duke Christian IV. He wanted a German breed similar to the English Thoroughbred. He built a royal stud, or breeding stable, to raise elegant horses.

WHERE DO THEY LIVE?

The home of this breed is the city of Zweibrücken in southwestern Germany.

Germany

Europe